Annie O'Hagan

Cuba at a Glance

Annie O'Hagan

Cuba at a Glance

ISBN/EAN: 9783337379209

Printed in Europe, USA, Canada, Australia, Japan

Cover: Foto ©Suzi / pixelio.de

More available books at **www.hansebooks.com**

CUBA
AT A GLANCE

BY

A. O'HAGAN
AND
E. B. KAUFMAN

WITH AN INTRODUCTION BY
President T. Estrada Palma
of the Cuban Junta

ЯHR

NEW YORK . R. H. RUSSELL
1808

THANKS are due the *New York Journal* for the use of its library and access to the letters of its war correspondents.

The authors also acknowledge their indebtedness to the Cuban Junta, whose original documents have been of great assistance.

Introduction

HISTORY proves that the independence of a people has always been born of sacrifice. In no instance, however, has there been such suffering, sacrifice and abnegation as was demanded of the Cuban people. From 1868, for ten long and bloody years, the Cubans engaged in an unequal struggle against Spain; unequal in numbers and unequal in resources. Not only the patriots in arms suffered, but their families and friends were sacrificed to the sanguinary brutality of the Spanish commanders.

At last, when almost exhausted, Spain offered terms, which were accepted but never fulfilled.

The spirit of independence only slumbered; the fires of patriotism still glowed.

On the 24th of February, 1895, the call to arms again sounded. It found response in the hearts of all true Cubans.

The veteran fighter was ready to make renewed sacrifices for the ideal. The youths sought to emulate the noble example of their sires.

The revolution was not entered upon blindly. Too well had the Cubans been taught what they had to expect from the soldiers of Spain. There would be no mercy for the patriot in arms, none for the sick or the wounded. Age and sex would not stay the hand of the Spaniard. The country would be ruined; all would have to be sacrificed.

Yet the Cubans never faltered. Rather have the country reduced to a heap of ashes than the mockery of the fertility of the land under Spanish rule.

The Cubans had not enjoyed the privileges of men. They toiled for the benefit of the Spanish tyrant and despoiler. They did not live; they existed.

From out of the ash heap they would form a new nation, ruled by the highest type of government—of, for and by the people. Enriched by patriotic blood, the island would become more productive than ever.

 · No more false promises were to be accepted. From the beginning the Cubans cut all bridges behind them. They adopted their motto— "Independence or Death."

How steadfast they have been in carrying out their resolve is now history.

Never has there been such suffering entailed on an entire people. So certain were the Spaniards of the sympathy of all Cubans with the revolution that they took measures to exterminate the entire race.

The half of our suffering and sacrifice is not known, the other half appeared so incredible that years passed before the world was convinced. Spain, a recognized nation, was listened to and believed. Cuba, having taken the law in her own hands, was looked upon with suspicion.

Only in the United States was there sympathy for the oppressed and the outraged.

The patriots in arms shed their blood freely; those in the cities and abroad coined their blood to supply arms and ammunition. But the sacrifice had not been uselessly made; the blood shed had not been in vain; the lives lost were not fruitless. Once satisfied of the true condition of affairs, the American people were not to be restrained. They fulfilled their mission on this continent, their duty to civilization and humanity.

The result is a most holy war.

One more republic is added to the American nations.

T. Estrada Palma.

Una carta de Máximo Gómez a Fitzhugh Lee

En campaña Febrero 20/98

Al General Mr Fitzhz Lee, Consul General de los Estados Unidos en la Habana.

General:

La noticia de la catástrofe del "Maine" nos ha afectado dolorosamente al pueblo cubano en armas y, en su nombre, tengo la honra de dirijirme á V. para expresarle la pena que en todos ha dejado, la pérdida de tantas vidas.

Los cubanos no olvidamos cuanto eximi debemos al pueblo de la Gran Nación que siente nuestros anhelos y comprende la justicia de nuestro sacrificio, permitame, pues, que le suplique haga llegar hasta el la expresión de nuestra fraternal condolencia por el triste hecho que lamentamos, y por mi parte, reciba mi pésame sentido y la espresion sincera de mi mas alta consideración y estima.

B. S. M. Ste

M. Gomez.

Es copia

Cuban Republic,
Army of Invasion,
2nd Commandent

Nueva Pass, Feb. 21, 1896.

To Delegate Thomas Estrada Palma,
New York.

My Distinguished Friend:

Señora Felicia Facenda, the wife of Col. Adel Castillo, accompanied by her daughter, being obliged to move to your city, I take great pleasure in recommending them with all consideration to you. I know that you will be pleased to show them all the politeness which they deserve on account of their relationship to their worthy chief, renowned for his patriotism, courage and excellent conduct, and also that they will receive such treatment from you as people deserve who leave their country to escape the persecutions and dangers due to the policy which Spain through Weyler has just inaugurated here. I speak for them their deep gratitude and I once more beg you to believe me

Your most obedient servant and friend who kisses your hand.

I shall refer to these
horrible things no further.

They are there; God
pity me, I have seen
them; they will remain
in my mind forever —
and this is almost the
twentieth century.

Christ died nineteen
hundred years ago, and
Spain is a christian nation.

She has set up more crosses
in more lands, beneath
more skies, and under
them has butchered more
people than all the other
nations of the earth combined

God grant that before
another Christmas morning
the last vestige of spanish
tyranny and oppression will
have vanished from the
western hemisphere

John M. Thurston.

Contents

I.

REMEMBER the Maine!
Release the reconcentrados!
One call is the cry for vengeance; one, the cry for humanity. Together they are the watchwords of the American-Spanish war of 1898. About them the causes of the conflict group themselves.

On the night of February 15, 1898, the United States battle ship Maine was blown up in Havana Harbor. The Maine was paying what is called in diplomatic language "a friendly visit." It lay in waters under the jurisdiction of a nation with which the United States was at peace.

The night was quiet, warm and starlit.

The seamen of the Maine who were off duty had, many of them, turned into their bunks. Some sat smoking their "goodnight pipes." Most of the officers had gone to their cabins. Some were writing letters.

At twenty minutes past nine a frightful

shock was felt. The ship was rent. In a few minutes the water was full of floating bodies, the air bright with flame. The Maine was destroyed, and with her two hundred and forty-six American seamen were hurled to swift death.

"I was just closing a letter to my family when I felt the crash of the explosion."

This was part of Captain Sigsbee's testimony given before the United States Naval Board of Inquiry, consisting of Captain W. T. Sampson, Captain T. E. Chadwick, Lieutenant W. P. Potter and Lieutenant Commander Adolph Marix.

"It was a bursting, rending and crashing sound or roar of immense volume, largely metallic in character. It was succeeded by a metallic sound, probably of falling debris, a trembling and lurching motion of the vessel, then an impression of subsidence, attended by an eclipse of the electric lights and intense darkness within the cabin. I knew immediately that the Maine had been blown up and that she was sinking. * * * Nearing the outer entrance I met Private Anthony, the orderly at the cabin door at the time. He ran in to me, as I remember, apologizing in some fashion, and reported to me that the ship had been blown up and was sinking."

Questioned as to the attitude of the Spanish officials in Havana previous to the explosion, Captain Sigsbee said:—

"My relations with the officials were outwardly cordial, and I had no ground for assuming that they were not really cordial. * * * There was one hostile demonstration by people afloat. It was the first Sunday after our arrival, on board a ferryboat densely crowded with people, both civil and military, who were returning to Havana from a bull fight in Regla. The demonstration consisted of yells, whistles, and apparently derisive calls emanating from about thirty or forty people at most. It was not general."

After he had been questioned concerning the position of the Maine, the regular inspection of its coal bunkers, of its inflammables and paints, its ash buckets, its electric plants, its magazines and shell rooms, the caution and the general discipline; and after Ensign W. V. N. Powelson, U. S. N., government divers and mining experts had also testified, "the Court found—that the loss of the Maine on the occasion named was not in any respect due to fault or negligence on the part of any of the officers of said vessel.

"In the opinion of the Court the Maine was destroyed by the explosion of a submarine mine, which caused the partial explosion of two or more of her forward magazines.

"The Court has been unable to obtain evidence fixing the responsibility for the destruction of the Maine upon any person or persons."

Sixty-six days after the loss of the battle ship and thirty-two days after the report of the Court, war was begun against Spain. Although the Court was unable to fix the responsibility, the nation at large did not hesitate to assume that burden. In the ultimatum that preceded the opening of hostilities there was no mention of the destruction of the two hundred and forty-six American sailors; still the battle cry of the war has been "Remember the Maine!"

The ultimatum sent to Spain on April 20, 1898, consisted of three parts. The first explained that the United States Congress demanded the evacuation of Cuba by the Spanish; the second, that the President had been directed by Congress to use the land and naval forces of the United States to enforce this de-

mand; and the third, that it was the President's duty to request an answer within forty-
eight hours.

Within forty-eight hours the ultimatum had
been rejected by the Cortes, and the United
States was pledged to free Cuba.

II.

THAT was the state of Cuba that the United States Congress should command Spain's evacuation?

Since October, 1896, 800,000 peaceful Cubans, country people, have been driven from their homes and herded in the adjacent towns and cities, their dwellings burnt behind them.

These were mainly women, children and old men.

Four hundred thousand of them have died by starvation.

The others are living skeletons, wandering through the towns begging. They are without money, without clothes, without tools and without strength.

This was the result of General Weyler's order of concentration. The Spanish commander had been annoyed by the aid given the insurgent Cubans by the non-combatant country people, the "pacificos." The rebels could count on food, clothing, horses and shelter from them.

By January, 1897, the country side was bare of asylums for the rebels and stripped of friends. The little thatch-roofed cottages of the peasants were in ashes.

In the towns the reconcentrados, as the concentrated pacificos are called, were allotted fields for cultivation. These fields were never large enough for raising a sufficient product to support life. The reconcentrados were allotted no tools and no seed. They had no money to buy them. The gift of the fields thus became a mockery. Famine and all the dread diseases that accompany it spread ruin through their ranks.

In July, 1897, the town of Chaseajaba contained two hundred and fifty reconcentrados. In October there were five left, three of them children.

In one month, December, 1897, 1,300 reconcentrados in Mantanzas—more than one-tenth of the whole number there—died.

In 1895 there were 60,000 Chinamen in Cuba. Now there are 10,000.

In November, 1897, after Blanco succeeded Weyler as Captain General of Cuba, he made a feint of modifying the concentration order. The victims, however, were already too weakened and diseased to profit by it.

Cuba was no more "the fairest land that eyes had ever looked upon."

Consular reports contained statistics of horrors. Sightseers told sickening tales of what they witnessed. Newspaper correspondents wrote columns descriptive of atrocities.

Writing in 1897, Richard Harding Davis describes a state of affairs in Cardenas:—

"I found the hospital for this colony behind three blankets which had been hung across a corner of the warehouse. A young woman and a man were lying side by side, the girl on a cot and the man on the floor. The others sat within a few feet of them on the other side of the blankets, apparently lost to all sense of their danger, and too dejected and hopeless to even raise their eyes when I gave them money.

"A fat little doctor was caring for the sick woman, and he pointed through the cracks in the floor at the green slime below us, and held his fingers to his nose and shrugged his shoulders. I asked him what ailed his patients, and he said it was yellow fever, and pointed again at the slime, which moved and bubbled in the hot sun.

"He showed me babies with the skin drawn so tightly over their little bodies that the bones showed through as plainly as the rings under a glove. They were covered with sores, and they protested as loudly as they could against the treatment which the world was giving them, clinching their fists and sobbing with pain when the sore places came in contact with their mothers' arms. A planter who had at one time employed a large number of these people, and who was moving about among them, said that five hundred had died in Cardenas since the order to leave the fields had been issued. Another gentleman told me that in the huts at the back of the town there had been twenty-five cases of smallpox in one week, of which seventeen had resulted in death.

* * *

"Thousands of human beings are now herded together around the seaport towns of Cuba, who cannot be fed, who have no knowledge of cleanliness or sanitation, who have no doctors to care for them and who cannot care for themselves.

"Many of them are dying of sickness, and some of starvation, and this is the healthy season. In April and May the rains will come, and the fever will thrive and spread, and cholera, yellow fever and smallpox will turn Cuba

into one huge plague spot, and the farmers'
sons whom Spain has sent over here to be
soldiers, and who are dying by the dozens before they have learned to pull the comb off a
bunch of cartridges, are going to die by the
hundreds, and women and children who are
innocent of any offense will die with them, and
there will be a quarantine against Cuba, and
no vessel can come into her ports or leave
them.

*   *   *

"In other wars men have fought with men,
and women have suffered indirectly because
the men were killed, but in this war it is the
women, herded together in the towns like cattle, who are going to die, while the men,
camped in the fields and the mountains, will
live."

A year later his testimony was practically
repeated by an official committee from Congress. A commission, composed of Senator
Thurston, of Nebraska, Senator Gallinger, of
New Hampshire, Senator Money of Mississippi, Representative Amos J. Cummings of
New York and Representative William Alden
Smith of Michigan, visited Cuba and told what
they saw. Their verdict was that "Weyler had

in the order of concentration devised a scheme
of human suffering and sorrow that put Dan-
te's 'Inferno' into the shade, and converted a
contented, prosperous people into a herd of
suffering, starving unfortunates."

Senator Gallinger reported that he was assured by Miss Barton, leader of the Red Cross
Relief Society, that the famine in Cuba was
ten thousand times worse than that which had
prevailed in India, Armenia or anywhere else.

Senator Thurston, in his impassioned appeal to the United States Senate on March 24,
said:—

"For myself, I went to Cuba firmly believing
the condition of affairs there had been greatly
exaggerated by the press, and my own efforts
were directed in the first instance to the attempted exposure of these supposed exagger-
ations.

"Mr. President, there has undoubtedly been
much sensationalism in the journalism of the
time, but as to the condition of affairs in Cuba
there has been no exaggeration because exaggeration has been impossible. * * * The
pictures in the American newspapers of the
starving reconcentrados are true. They can
all be duplicated by the thousands. I never

saw, and please God I may never again see, so deplorable a sight as the reconcentrados in the suburbs of Matanzas. I can never forget to my dying day the hopeless anguish in their despairing eyes. Huddled about their little bark huts, they raised no voice of appeal to us for alms as we went among them.

"The government of Spain has not and will not appropriate one dollar to save these people. They are now being attended and nursed and administered to by the charity of the United States. Think of the spectacle! We are feeding these citizens of Spain; we are nursing their sick; we are saving such as can be saved; and yet there are those who still say, 'It is right for us to send food, but we must keep our hands off.' I say that the time has come when muskets ought to go with the food."

III.

THE condition of the reconcentrados as thus outlined might seem a sentimental cause of war. But the interest of the United States in Cuba has for a long time been more than sentimental because of the vast commercial relations between the two countries. It has been more than merely neighborly, because through her ill government of Cuba Spain has involved us in difficulties which give us just cause for complaint.

When, after nearly half a century of turmoil and insurrection in Cuba, it became evident to the United States that the tranquillity necessary for prosperous trade could not be maintained under Spanish rule, our purchase of the island was discussed. This was in 1848.

The proposition met with warm support in the South, which, fearful of the growing influence of the North and West, was anxious to increase the slaveholding area of the United States. President Polk made overtures to Spain for the purchase of Cuba for $100,000,000, which Spain declined.

From this time Spain's attitude toward the United States in regard to Cuba was distinctly unfriendly. The affair of the Black Warrior in 1850 showed the hostile spirit.

The Black Warrior, a steamer owned in New York, was accustomed, in making monthly trips between New York and Mobile, to touch at Havana to leave and receive mail and passengers, but not to discharge or take on freight. She had been given, in April, 1847, a paper signed by Cuban authorities relieving her of the necessity of exhibiting at each landing a manifest of her cargo. In spite of this permit she was arrested in 1850 in Havana Harbor for having an undeclared cargo on board, although she had thirty-six times previously entered under the same conditions with the consent of the revenue officers. The cargo was seized and put on shore and the vessel fined. Captain Bullock, commanding officer, refused to pay the fine and entered a formal protest against the seizure. For this outrage Spain was eventually forced to pay the Black Warrior's owners $300,000.

This incident is illustrative of the system of

petty annoyances to which Spain subjected America. It included the search of American vessels by Spanish cruisers on the high seas and the arrest of American citizens in Cuba on trumped-up political charges.

Our Ministers to England, France, Spain— 'James Buchanan, J. G. Mason and Pierre Soule—held, in 1854, a conference to propose a plan to our State Department which should end our difficulties. Their scheme was set forth in the Ostend Manifesto. In it they declared:—

"We have arrived at the conclusion, and are thoroughly convinced, that an immediate and earnest effort ought to be made by the government of the United States to purchase Cuba from Spain at any price for which it can be obtained, not exceeding the sum of $120,-000,000.

"The Union can never enjoy repose nor possess reliable security as long as Cuba is not embraced within its boundaries.

"Its immediate acquisition by our government is of paramount importance, and we cannot doubt that it is a consummation devoutly wished for by its inhabitants.

"The intercourse which its proximity to our

coast begets and encourages between them and the citizens of the United States has in the progress of time so united their interests and blended their fortunes that they now look upon each other as if they were one people and had but one destiny."

*   *   *

"Cuba has thus become to us an unceasing danger and a permanent cause of anxiety and alarm."

*   *   *

"After we have offered Spain a price for Cuba far beyond its present value and this shall have been refused, it will then be time to consider the question, 'Does Cuba in the possession of Spain seriously endanger our internal peace and the existence of our cherished Union?'

"Should this question be answered in the affirmative, then by every law, human and divine, we shall be justified in wresting it from Spain if we possess the power; and this upon the very same principle that would justify an individual in tearing down the burning house of his neighbor if there were no other means of preventing the flames from destroying his own home."

Any action which the United States might have taken upon this manifesto was indefinitely deferred by the increase of her own political agitations, which finally culminated in the Civil War.

By the time the United States had ended the Civil War and re-established peace. the Cubans were engaged in their ten years' struggle against Spain. During this occurred two events, one shocking to humanity and civilization, one a direct outrage upon America. The first was "The Affair of the Students." The tomb of a member of the Cuban Volunteers, the powerful militia organization of Spanish loyalists in Havana, had been defaced. Suspicion pointed to the students of Havana University. Forty-three of these young men were tried for the offense on the complaint of the Volunteers, and were acquitted. The Volunteers then induced the Governor General to order a retrial, at which two-thirds of the jury should be from their own number. This court, of course, condemned the accused. Eight were sentenced to be shot, and on November 27, 1871, 15,000 Volunteers assembled to do the shooting.

Two years later came the Virginius outrage. The Virginius was a steamer chartered as belonging to John F. Patterson, an American citizen. She flew the American colors and was cleared as an American merchantman. She cruised in the Caribbean Sea. In October, 1873, she was seen off the coast of Cuba. She was chased by the Spanish cruiser Tornado along the coast of Santiago. On November 1st she was captured and brought into the port of Santiago de Cuba as a pirate ship. Of her hundred and fifty-five passengers forty-five had Anglo-Saxon names, the rest Spanish. But Captain Joseph Fry claimed for all protection as American citizens. Not only did he, but also E. G. Schmitt, vice-consul at Santiago, protest against the detention of the vessel. Mr. Schmitt's communications to the Governor of the province were disregarded and he himself virtually insulted. His messages were left unanswered, because, the Governor said, "Being engaged, as well as every one else, in meditation of the divine mysteries of All Saints' and the commemoration of All Souls' days, as prescribed by our holy religion, it was impossible for me until early this morning to comply with your wishes."

Mr. Schmitt was also refused the use of the marine cable to consult, as he desired, with the United States Consul at Kingston. Fifty-three of the Virginius' party were executed, among them Captain Fry. After being shot down, their bodies were beheaded, and the heads were displayed on spikes, while their trunks were trampled on by horses.

The night before his miserable death Captain Fry wrote his wife an interesting description of Spanish etiquette.

"I have been tried to-day, and the President of the Court Martial asked me the favor of embracing me at parting and clasped me to his heart. * * * Each of my judges and the secretary of the court and interpreter have promised me as a special favor to attend my execution. * * * I am told that my death will be painless; in short, I have had a very pleasant and cheerful chat about my funeral, to which I shall go in a few hours from now. * * * It is curious to see how I make friends. The priest who gave me communion this morning put a double scapula about my neck. A young Spanish officer brought me a bright new silk badge with the Blessed Virgin stamped upon it to wear to my execution for him and a handsome cross in some fair lady's handiwork. He embraced me affectionately with tears in his eyes.   *   *   *"

Then, even as in these latter days, an American newspaper correspondent, George Sherman, for trying to sketch the execution scene, was punished with imprisonment.

How far the slaughter of the Virginius' passengers would have continued but for the action of the British war ship Niobe it is impossible to say. The Niobe, under Sir Hampton Lorraine, sailed from Kingston, Jamaica, to Santiago and threatened to bombard the town if the outrages were not immediately stopped. Indignation throughout the United States was intense, and diplomatic relations between it and Spain were almost ruptured. General Sickles, the United States Minister at Madrid, demanded his passports, but Spain backed down, and the Virginius, with the remainder of her passengers, was surrendered to the United States. Indemnities were paid to families of the American subjects who had suffered death at Santiago.

This was not the only maritime difficulty between Spain and this country during the Ten Years' War. In 1877 the Ellen Rizpah, the Rising Sun, and the Edward Lee, all flying

the American flag and engaged in their legitimate pursuits outside of Cuban waters, were
fired upon by a Spanish war ship and detained
for days with circumstances of peculiar hard-
ship and brutality. Spain was forced to pay
an aggregate indemnity of $10,000 to their
owners.

In 1875 both President Grant and Secretary
of State Fish made statements concerning our
difficulties with Spain.

President Grant, in his message to Congress in 1875, refers to the American interests as follows:—

"The property of our citizens in Cuba is
large and is rendered insecure and depreciated
in value and in capacity of production by the
continuance of the strife and the unnatural
mode of its conduct."

Secretary Fish, in a letter to Caleb Cushing,
then Minister to Spain, wrote:—

"This struggle (the Ten Years' War) has
disturbed our tranquillity and commerce, has
called upon us not infrequently to witness bar-
barous violations of the rules of civilized warfare, and compelled us, for the sake of humanity, to raise our voice by way of protest.

"The world is witnessing on the part of the
insurgents, whom Spain still claims as sub-

jects, and for whose acts, as subjects, Spain must be held accountable in the judgment of the world, a warfare, not of the legitimate strife of relative force and strength, but of pillage and incendiarism, the burning of estates and sugar mills, the destruction of the means of production and of the wealth of the island.

"The United States purchases more largely than any other people of the productions of the island of Cuba, and therefore, more than any other for this reason, and still more by reason of its immediate neighborhood, is interested in the arrest of a system of wanton destruction which disgraces the age and affects every commercial people on the face of the globe.

"The United States has exerted itself to the utmost, for seven years, to repress unlawful acts on the part of self exiled subjects of Spain, relying on the promise of Spain to pacify the island. Seven years of strain on the powers of this government to fulfil all that the most exacting demands that one government can make, under any doctrine or claim of international obligation, upon another, have not witnessed the much hoped for pacification. The United States feels itself entitled to be relieved of this strain."

IV.

THE "unlawful acts" on the part of Spain's subjects to which the letter of Secretary Fish referred meant, of course, the conspiracies of Cubans hatched in the United States, the raising of forces and the collection of materials for insurrection here. Briefly, the United States had to perform detective and policeman duty for Spain to prevent the setting out of filibustering expeditions to Cuba. During the present war of Cuba against Spain the duty has been as irksome as it was in Grant's administration, and it has sometimes led to serious international complications.

In March, 1895, the Allianca, bound from Colon to New York, following the customary track for vessels near the Cuban shore, but outside the three-mile limit, was fired upon by a Spanish gunboat. The United States protest was this time immediately heeded and the act disavowed by Spain.

In April, 1896, the schooner Competitor,

with twenty-five or thirty men and a cargo of
arms and ammunition for the rebels, sailed
from Key West for Havana. On the coast of
Cuba, about sixty miles west of that part, the
Spanish launch Mensejara captured the
schooner. Some of the filibusters had already
landed. Others tried to swim ashore. Two of
these were killed. Alfred Laborde, an American, was captured on a reef which he had
gained. Four men—two Cubans, Bedia and
Maza; an Englishman, James Kildea, and an
American, a Jacksonville newspaper correspondent, Owen Milton—were captured on
the ship. They were court-martialed and sentenced to be shot.

A storm of protest arose. England and the
United States demanded civil trials for their
subjects. Captain-General Weyler raged at
the interference with his authority, but Prime
Minister Canovas, in Madrid, granted the stay
of execution required by England and America. Eventually the men were all released.
That occurred on January 23, 1897, "the
King's Saint Day," when all American political prisoners in Cuba were liberated under
promise to give no further aid to the insurgents.

The Competitor prisoners formed but a small part of the American colony in Cuba's jails at various times during the troubled years since the outbreak of the war, in 1894. Jules Sanguilly, a native Cuban but a naturalized American since 1878, was arrested in February, 1895, charged with rebellion. He was found guilty and sentenced to life imprisonment. In February, 1897, he was pardoned on the condition that he should leave the island.

Gaspar Betancourt, a naturalized American, was charged in January, 1897, with aiding the rebels, imprisoned 288 hours in solitary confinement, contrary to treaty, and was finally released in February, 1897.

Frank Agramonte, of New York, was arrested in May, 1895, charged with conspiracy against Spain. Secure in innocence and confident of acquittal, he gave himself up. For two years he was imprisoned at Santiago de Cuba without trial. He did not obtain his freedom until October, 1897.

A companion of Agramonte—Thomas Sainz—had suffered in the same way on the same charge.

The Rev. Albert Diaz and his brother were

arrested on April 16, 1896, tried and deported
to the United States on April 22.

American citizens having possessions or bus-
iness in Cuba suffered also under the Weyler
regime.

In September, 1896, Peter E. Rivery, an
American planter having a coffee estate near
St. Luis, in Pinar del Rio province, had his
property partly destroyed and was himself
threatened with death by Spanish troops.

William and Louis A. Glean, owners of a
sugar estate in Sagua la Grande, were arrested
in September, 1896, and thrown into prison
without being allowed to communicate with
the American Consul, with lawyers or with
witnesses. They were charged with keeping
arms for the insurgents. Their servants were
tortured to induce them to testify against their
employers—a device which failed. While they
were in prison their estate was burned by
Spanish troops, so that at the time of their
release they were practically penniless.

Henry W. McDonnell, of Alabama, a planter owning a plantation also near Havana, visited his property in Cuba in February, 1897.
Finding that his possessions had suffered considerably at the hands of the Spanish soldiers,

he criticized Spanish methods with great
frankness. He was immediately hauled before the authorities, his passports seized by
General Weyler and he himself arrested. He
was finally released at the demand of Consul
General Lee.

Most tragic of all was the death of Dr. Ri-
cardo Ruiz, an American dentist. He was arrested early in February, 1897, on the charge
of being a rebel sympathizer. He was thrown
into a foul cell in a suburban Havana jail and
was not permitted intercourse with counsel or
with his family for thirteen days. The requests
of Consul General Lee for information concerning the charges on which Ruiz was held
were ignored or evasively answered. On the
fourteenth day after his imprisonment he was
found dead. It was obvious that he had been
tortured to obtain a confession after the usual
Spanish method and that his death was the result of the treatment.

These and similar outrages against American citizens in Cuba led to the filing in April,
1898, of claims against Spain for $16,000,000
damages for personal injury, imprisonment,
loss of stock, burning of sugar plantations, &c.

Within the last two years, for the high

crime of giving authentic information to the American press, the following American newspaper correspondents were arrested, imprisoned or deported:

William Mannix, Sylvester Scovel, Charles Michelson, Lorenzo Betancourt, Elbert Rappelje, James Creelman, Frederick W. Lawrence, William W. Gay, Thomas R. Dawley, C. B. Pendleton, Theodore Pous and George Bronson.

Charles Govin, a correspondent for a Florida paper, was brutally murdered by the Spanish troops under Colonel Ochoa, into whose hands he fell after they had had an engagement with the Cubans. His passports and his correspondent's certificate were examined, thrown aside, and at a wave of Ochoa's hand Govin was bound and riddled with bullets.

V.

JUANA, Fernandina, Santiago, Ave Maria—thus was the Island of Cuba successively christened by the Spaniards.

"Cuba" itself is from Cubanan. It means what it has always been to the Spanish—the place of gold.

1492, the discovery of America, is also the date of the discovery of Cuba. For four centuries the Island of Cuba has been governed by the Cortes of Madrid—7,000 miles away. Not until 1511, however, did the Spanish think it worth while to colonize. They did not establish a settlement there until they thought they had exhausted the wealth of the neighboring island of Hayti. Then, believing there was no more gold in Hayti's mines, they sent a band of 300 men under Diego Velasquez to make a settlement in Cuba.

Diego Velasquez and his men found the natives peaceable, happy and contented and under the government of nine independent chiefs. As Columbus wrote to Ferdinand and Isabella after his first experience with the West Indians: "The people are so affectionate, so tractable and so peaceable that I swear to Your Highnesses that there is not a better race of men nor a better country in the world. They love their neighbor as themselves; their conversation is the sweetest and mildest in the world, cheerful and always accompanied by a smile. And, although it is true that they go naked, yet Your Highnesses may be assured they have many commendable customs."

The reputation gained by the Spaniards in 1511 has never been forfeited. It was then that Hatuey, a native chieftain, who had opposed the Dons, was tied to a stake with fagots piled about him. While the flames rose a Franciscan monk held a crucifix before him and told him the beauties of the Christian faith.

"Be sorry for your sins," he cried, "and gain a place in heaven."

"Where is heaven?" asked Hatuey, "and are there Spaniards there?"

The priest answered that there were many.

"Then," cried Hatuey, "pray let me go somewhere else."

The subjugation of the natives by Velasquez was quick. Without the loss of a man he took possession of the island—a possession that has endured almost uninterruptedly for nearly four centuries.

The natives were allotted to the settlers in gangs of about three hundred to each Spaniard. They were employed in the cultivation of the soil, but it was soon found that they were not strong enough for such field work as the colonists would have imposed upon them.

Negro slaves from Spain, where for a considerable time slavery had existed, were therefore imported.

The first settlement established by the Spaniards was Santiago, on the southeast coast, for a long time Cuba's capital. The next was Trinidad, on the eastern shore. San Cristobal de la Habana was the third, founded in 1515. It is now called Batabano and is directly opposite Havana on the eastern coast.

Four years later the name of Havana was given to the present capital.

One of the first Governors sent by Spain to this colony was Hernando de Soto, famed in

American history as the discoverer of the Mississippi.

In 1538 Havana had been set on fire by a French privateer. To guard against the repetition of such a disaster, de Soto erected a fortress. It was called the Castillo de la Fuerza.

In 1553 Havana, which had gained considerably in importance by the transfer of the Governor's residence from Santiago, was attacked and partially destroyed by the French.

A year later it was plundered by pirates.

In 1585, being again seriously menaced by the English, under Drake, two more fortresses were built. They were named the Bateria de la Punta and the Castillo del Morro. These still guard the entrance to Havana.

During the reign of Philip III. the sugar and tobacco industries grew in importance in Cuba. This was due to the expulsion of the Moors from Spain and the consequent cessation of their cultivation in Spain.

During all this period Spain imposed heavy trade restriction upon Cuba. The island could sell its products to no other country. It could buy what it needed from no other country. Seville was the only Spanish port with which the island was allowed to trade. The natural result was extensive smuggling carried on between the colonists and foreign adventurers.

The men with whom Cuba carried on this illegal commerce had their headquarters in the bays of Hayti, which had been almost deserted by that time for the more attractive country of Cuba. The Haytians who were left lived mainly on the flesh of cattle, which they smoked by a peculiar process called bucanning. The smugglers, copying this way of preserving meat for use on shipboard, came to be known as "buccaneers."

For over 150 years these buccaneers harrassed the Spanish. They were encouraged by all other nations antagonistic to the Spanish. They were even commissioned by other countries as privateers. They sailed the Spanish main—the waters surrounding the West Indies—stopping Spanish ships and interfering with Spanish commerce. When in 1655 England gained Jamaica they grew even more daring and more powerful. Jamaica became the headquarters, whence they issued not only to plunder vessels upon the high seas, but even to ravage the cities and the mainland of Cuba. In 1671 one of them—Henry Morgan—was knighted by Great Britain for his exploits.

As a protection in the midst of the depreda-
tions of this gentry Havana was fortified by
walls. The magnificent harbor could only be
entered by stealth or by force. In 1697 the
European Powers set the seal of general con-
demnation upon the buccaneers. The Cuban settlements revived materially and grew
in importance.

In 1713 the opening of the new era in Spain
by the ending of the Hapsburg rule and the
establishment of the Bourbons was felt in Cuba. The agricultural wealth had begun to
make a showing. A new policy was adopted.
The tobacco trade was made a royal monopoly. Out of this measure a serious clashing
between the colonists and the mother country ensued. The monoply was violently opposed. Constant friction and bloody encoun-
ters between the Cuban and the Spanish militia were engendered. Systematic smuggling,
mainly by British traders in Jamaica, again
resulted. Another Anglo-Spanish war followed and ended in a general European one.

In the thirteen years of peace that followed
the cessation of hostilities in 1748 smuggling
in Cuba grew beyond control and Spain was
forced to give up the tobacco monopoly.

British power grew in America.   France
and Spain were anxiously jealous of England,
and Cuba felt that at any moment she might
become a scene of depredation in the general
conflict of European nations.

VI.

IN 1762 Cuba's expectations were realized. Havana was besieged by the English.

All Europe, practically, was involved in the struggle known as the Seven Years' War. In January of 1762 hostilities were declared against Spain. In the summer Lord Albermarle was sent against Havana with a fleet of 200 ships and a force of 14,041 men.

In this force were some whose names appear later in the pages of American history. The British Colonies in America contributed their share of soldiers for the siege. Lawrence Washington, a brother of George, served in the expedition. New Jersey, New York and Connecticut sent 2,300 men. General Lyman and Israel Putnam were among them, the latter gaining military training which afterward proved valuable to him when he took up arms against the British. The American loss was heavy. Few of the Colonial troops, either officers or men, ever returned. Most of those whom the Spanish guns spared were killed by sickness.

The defence was stubbornly conducted. Spain had a force of 27,610 men in the city. Among them was a body which has been a feature of military life in Cuba ever since that time—the Cuban Volunteers. This organization has always been allied with the Spanish party in Cuba. At the time of the British siege there was, of course, no other party. The brilliant work of the Volunteers during this obstinate ten months' struggle gave them their first glory.

In spite of the larger force of the Spanish, the English were successful. The captors seized $3,680,925, which was divided among them.

During the English occupation of Cuba the island enjoyed the first progressive and liberal rule it had known. Its ports were opened to free commerce.

The sanitary condition of Havana had been up to that time a disgrace to even the primitive sanitary science of the age. Under the English rule improvements were begun which, if they had been continued, might have left the region free in great part from the yellow fever plague which menaces the island each year, and which is due largely to municipal uncleanliness.

Roads were opened up all over the island. An era of modern prosperity seemed almost begun, when Spain again became owner of Cuba, the Pearl of the Antilles.

This happened in February, 1763. England gave Cuba back to Spain in return for Florida.

But it was impossible for Spanish rule to undo the good work of the English completely and at once. One of the first Governors under the new Spanish regime happened—and this was an unusual occurrence—to have the interests of the Cubans at heart as much as those of Spain. He was Luis de Las Casas. He was made Governor in 1790. He encouraged trade with the young Republic just established in America. It was about this time that sugar became an important article of trade, though not even then universally used. It was sold at forty-three cents a pound, a price which prohibited its use in large quantities. But it was becoming a large factor in commercial relations, and the generous policy of Las Casas toward the United States helped largely in developing the industry in Cuba.

Another act that endeared Las Casas to Americans was the removal of the body of Columbus from Hayti, where it had been entombed, and the placing of it in Havana Cathedral.

Las Casas was succeeded in 1796 by the Count of Santa Clara. He also proved to be a man of just and liberal ideas. Most of the fortifications which guard the island now were erected by him. The Bateria de Santa Clara, outside Havana, was built by him and named in his honor.

Perhaps it was a result of the beneficent policies of these two Goverors that Cuba became confirmed in her allegiance to Spain. When Napoleon in 1808 deposed the Bourbon King, Ferdinand VII., and placed his own brother, Joseph, on the Spanish throne, every member of the Provincial Council of Cuba declared unwaveringly loyalty to the old dynasty. For this it was called "The Ever Faithful Isle," a title which has proved its only reward for its allegiance, although a more substantial one was promised at the time by the Provisional Government at Seville. This body, acting for the deposed Bourbons, promised that all Spanish subjects everywhere should have equal rights.

How the promise to "The Ever Faithful Isle" was kept is an interesting lesson in Spanish diplomacy.

VII.

CHAPTER VII.

IN 1813 Bonaparte Joseph was deposed and Ferdinand VII. was restored to Spain. He began his new rule by ignoring the constitution, dissolving the Cortes and making himself an absolute monarch. The American colonies felt his despotic yoke again.

In 1809 and 1810 Buenos Ayres, Venezuela and Peru started rebellions against Spanish authority, which ended after several years in their complete independence. The Spanish loyalists from these countries flocked to Cuba and expected to be retainers of the Crown at Cuba's expense. Then Spain attempted to make Cuba a military station from which she could direct operations against the new republics, which she wished to reconquer. The troops sent for this purpose to Cuba disliked their mission, the colonists were ill-satisfied with the government, and the general discontent gave birth to numerous secret political societies. The insurrections planned by these associations soon aroused the interest of the United States in Cuban affairs.

The first open revolt was in 1820. Its leaders proclaimed as the governing law of Cuba the liberal constitution granted by the Provisional Government of Seville when Ferdinand was deposed. It took two years of discord and rebellion to force the King to yield.

The next revolution planned was that of the Soles de Bolivar, in 1823. It purposed to establish a Cuban republic. The rising was to take place simultaneously in several cities on the island, but the purposes of the society became known to the government, and on the very day when independence was to be declared the leaders were imprisoned.

In 1825 the King, possibly to discourage revolution, defined the powers of the Captain Generals of Cuba in this way: he gave to them "the fullest authority to send away from the island any persons in office, whatever their occupation, rank, class or condition, whose continuance therein they might deem injurious, or whose conduct, public or private, might alarm them, replacing them with persons faithful to His Majesty."

As a result of this the "Black Eagle Society" formed a second invading expedition, with headquarters in Mexico, and recruiting agencies in the United States. Again the ringleaders were caught by the Spanish authorities, as their predecessors of the Soles de Bolivar had been.

In 1844 occurred an uprising so barbarously quelled by Spain as to show that she had not left behind her the days of the Inquisition. The slaves on the sugar plantations about Matanzas were suspected of being ready to revolt. Absolute proof being lacking, they were tortured for evidence. One thousand three hundred and forty-six persons were tried by Inquisition methods and convicted. Seventy-eight were shot; punishment of various degrees was inflicted upon the others.

The next conspiracy was headed by Narciso Lopez, a native Venezuelan, who had served in the Spanish army. In 1848 he started a revolutionary movement which was unsuccessful. He escaped to New York, bringing many of his allies with him. There he succeeded in augmenting the sympathy already aroused and in establishing a movement for practical aid. In 1849 he attempted to return to Cuba with a small party, but was intercepted by the United States authority. A year later, having organized his forces outside of United States jurisdiction, he succeeded in reaching Cuba with 600 men. In spite of his persistency he was compelled to re-embark and was chased by a Spanish war ship to Key West, where his party disbanded.

Still undaunted by failure, the next year found Lopez starting from New Orleans for Cuba with a regiment of 450 men. Second in command to himself was Colonel Crittenden, of Kentucky, a West Point man, who had won his title in the Mexican War. Landing in Cuba, the forces were divided, 130 men under Crittenden remaining on the shore to guard the supplies, while Lopez with the rest pushed on into the interior. Both parties were surrounded by the Spanish. Crittenden's force, when it had been reduced to fifty men, was captured and destroyed. Lopez and his detachment were all captured, and Lopez himself shot.

This attempt aroused the greatest sympathy in this country, both on account of Lopez, who had become well known, and because of the death of Crittenden.

An expedition led by General Quitman, of Mississippi, two years later, to assist Cuban patriots, seemed to have a chance of success because of its adequate supply of men and arms, but the United States interfered. The American expedition was abandoned and the native patriots shot.

The details of these revolts were not without importance to the United States. They interfered with our commercial interests in Cuba, which had grown large. They forced us to be on guard against Cuban conspirators and against filibustering expeditions. But the most important result of Spain's determination to use Cuba as a ground for the reconquering of her former American possessions was the formulation of the Monroe Doctrine. In 1823 France and Spain formed what they were pleased to term a Holy Alliance, with the object of resubjugating the Spanish possessions. President Monroe said that "any attempt by a European power to gain dominion in America would be regarded by the United States as an unfriendly act." England, by her recognition of the Spanish-American republics, reinforced the United States in her attitude, and thus the Monroe Doctrine became established as a feature of international law.

VIII.

SPAIN, in 1868, was in the throes of an internal struggle, in the course of which Queen Isabella was forced to flee. Cuba did not then, as she had done sixty years before, when Napoleon deposed the Bourbons, proclaim her loyalty to her sovereigns. She had learned how Spain rewarded loyalty, and she took advantage of the trouble in the Peninsula to begin a revolution on the island as the only means by which she could obtain redress for her grievances.

Her grievances were many. In the Edinburgh Review of 1873 they were stated as follows:—

"Spain governs the island of Cuba with an iron and blood-stained hand. The former holds the latter deprived of political, civil and religious liberties. Hence the unfortunate Cubans being illegally prosecuted and sent into exile, or executed by military commissions in times of peace; hence their being kept from

public meetings, and forbidden to speak or
write on affairs of State; hence their remon-
strances against the evils that afflict them being looked upon as the proceedings of rebels,
from the fact that they are obliged to keep si-
lence and obey; hence the never-ending plague
of hungry officials from Spain to devour the
product of their industry and labor; hence
their exclusion from the art of government;
hence, the restrictions to which public in-
struction with them is subjected in order to
keep them so ignorant as not to be able to
know and enforce their rights in any shape
or form whatever; hence the navy and the
standing army, which are kept in their country at an enormous expenditure from their
own wealth to make them bend their knees
and submit their necks to the iron yoke that
disgraces them; hence the grinding taxation
under which they labor and which would
make them all perish in misery but for the
marvellous fertility of their soil."

The annual revenue demanded by Spain
from Cuba up to the time of the beginning of
the war was about $26,000,000. This rev-
enue, of course, was not used to Cuba's advantage. The Captain General—always a

Spaniard—received a salary of $50,000 a year, with perquisites; the provincial governors—always Spaniards—$12,000 each, with perquisites; the two archbishops—always Spaniards —$18,000, with perquisites. As will be seen, there was no chance for native Cubans. Even the lowest offices were given by Spanish politicians to their friends. Naturally great bitterness between the Insulars, or native Cubans, and the Peninsulars, or Spaniards in Cuba, was aroused.

Spain still had almost a monopoly of trade to Cuba and forced the Cubans to pay the highest taxes on all the necessities of life. Wheaten bread, under the heavy duty imposed on flour, ceased to be an article of common diet on the island.

An unheard of rate was charged on postage, so that a native Cuban receiving a prepaid letter at his own door had to pay 37 1-2 cents additional postage.

While the Spaniards paid $3.23 per capita of interest on their national debt, the Cubans paid $6.39, although they had some of its benefits.

In 1868, when it was proposed still further to tax them, they rose in arms. On October

10th Carlos M. de Cespedes, a lawyer of Bayamo, with 128 poorly equipped men, issued a declaration of independence on the plantation of Yara, and within a few weeks he was at the head of 10,000 men, badly armed but determined. By April, 1869, a constitution for a republican form of government was drawn up. It provided for a president, vice president, cabinet and a legislature. It abolished slavery, and under it Cespedes was elected president, Francisco Aguilero vice president, and a legislature convened.

The war had been in progress six months, the advantages being with the insurgents under General Quesada. Every Cuban who did fall into the hands of the Spaniards was shot on the spot. The Spanish General, the Count of Valmaseda, issued a proclamation outlining his plan of warfare. He said:—

"The reinforcements of troops that I have been waiting for have arrived. With them I shall give protection to the good and punish promptly all those that still remain in rebellion against the government of the metropolis.

"1st.—Every man, from the age of fifteen years upward, found away from his habitation, who does not prove a justified motive therefor, will be shot.

"2d.—Every habitation unoccupied will be burned by the troops.

"3d.—Every habitation from which does not float a white flag as a signal that its occupants desire peace will be reduced to ashes.

"Women that are not living at their own homes or at the houses of their relatives will collect in the town of Jiguane or Bayamo, where maintenance will be provided. Those who do not present themselves will be conducted forcibly."

This proclamation raised a gale of protest among civilized nations, but nevertheless these were the Spanish tactics throughout the war.

Until 1871 the insurgents kept the field with a force of about fifty thousand men. They were constantly victorious in engagements, but the Spanish resources were greater, and finally the insurgents were driven into a sort of guerilla-like warfare. There were roving bands of insurgents that harassed and damaged, but did not actually meet the Spanish troops. The Cuban climate proved an active ally of the Cubans in disposing of the enemy. The war became a desultory sort of struggle. By 1876 145,000 soldiers and Spain's best commanders had been sent to Cuba and had not yet subdued the rebels, who were invincible in the eastern part of the island, although they could take no cities. Cuban crops had been ruined and Cuban trade decreased. Spain had wasted money and men, losing about eighty thousand of her land forces. Taxes had been trebled. By 1878 both sides were ready for peace, which was the result of promised compromise and concessions rather than of victory on either side.

General Martinez de Campos, who was the Spanish commander at that time, made overtures to the Cubans under Maximo Gomez. The result was the treaty of El Zanjon, February 10, 1878. This treaty promised Cuba representation in the Spanish Cortes and granted a general pardon to all who had taken any part, directly or indirectly, in the revolutionary movement.

IX.

THE most important element in the treaty of El Zanjon promised Cuba representation in the Cortes at Madrid. The promise was kept in the letter and utterly broken in the spirit. The Peninsulars soon obtained absolute control of the polls, and invariably elected a majority of the deputies. Such representatives naturally did not have the interests of Cuba at heart, and no legislation to its advantage was undertaken.

The cities, hopelessly in debt, were unable to provide sewerage, garbage service or street cleaning. Schools were closed. There was, and is, but one asylum for the insane in Cuba, that in Havana. Elsewhere, the insane are confined in prison cells. Church and state holidays take up one-third of the time that might be devoted to labor to meet public expenses.

Not only did Cuba, out of the earnings of the other two-thirds of the year, have to pay the high salaries of her horde of Spanish rulers, but she suffered enormously from the dishonesty of those officials. The custom house frauds alone, between 1878 and 1895, amounted to $100,000,000. But no relief was to be obtained under the Spanish interpretation of the Zanjon treaty. Patience ceased to seem a virtue, and in 1894 a new insurrection was mapped out by Jose Marti.

He organized his first expedition in New York, and set sail for Cuba with three vessels, the Lagonda, the Amadis and the Baracoa, containing men and war materials. The expedition was stopped by United States authorities. Later, Marti joined Gomez, Crombet, Guerra and the Maceo brothers—all insurgents in the Ten Years' War—in Santo Domingo, Gomez's home. They did not reach Cuba Cuba until May, 1895, but, in the preceding February, the insurgents had begun their rebellion, and they gained ground even before the arrival of their commanders.

The war has been conducted largely on the same principles as was the Ten Years' War. The insurgents seldom risk an open battle; the Spaniards gain but little ground in opposing the guerilla methods of the Cubans. On May 19th Marti was killed in a skirmish. Go-

mez took command in his place, and thus the
war practically began with the leaders on each
side the same men who had closed the last war,
General Martinez Campos and Maximo
Gomez. Gomez has remained at the head of
his forces. Campos was replaced in February,
1896, by General Valeriano Weyler, who was,
in turn, recalled in October, 1897, for Don
Ramon Blanco. During the interval between
the departure of Campos and the arrival of
Weyler, General Marin was in charge.

Under Commander-in-Chief Gomez the
Cubans were in six divisions, operating in the
six provinces:—In Pinar del Rio Antonio
Maceo commanded; in Havana, General
Aguerre; in Matanzas, Lacret; in Las Villas,
Carillo; in Camaguey, Suarez; in Oriento,
Jose Maceo. Jose Maceo died, and Antonio
Maceo was afterward killed. Saurez was cash-
iered for cowardice, and Garcia later replaced
him in the East.

The most important battle of the Campos
campaign was that of Bayamo. In July, 1895,
Campos met the rebels. The Spaniards were
severely tried, and Campos' life was saved only
by the sacrifice of that of General Santocildes.
Antonio Maceo treated the wounded whom

the Spanish left on the field, at the time of their retreat, with the utmost humanity. He wrote to Campos:—

"To His Excellency the General Martinez Campos:—

"Dear Sir—Anxious to give careful and efficient attendance to the wounded Spanish soldiers that your troops left behind on the battle field, I have ordered that they be lodged in the houses of the Cuban families that live nearest to the battle grounds until you send for them.

"With my assurance that the forces you may send to escort them back will not meet any hostile demonstrations from my soldiers, I have the honor to be, sir,

"Yours respectfully,
"ANTONIO MACEO."

After this Campos retreated, but the Cubans continued their invasion toward the interior. In July, 1895, Gomez issued a proclamation from Camaguey, prohibiting the carrying of articles of commerce into cities of Spanish occupation, and, under threat of direst penalty, the cultivation, cutting or grinding of sugar cane. The Spaniards at first regarded this as a humorous document. But they soon had cause to change their views.

When Campos failed to confine the insurgents to the East, he arranged a snare for them near Mal Tiempo. There the Spanish were caught in their own trap. The Cubans were victorious.

Again Campos tried to hem them in. In December, 1895, he lay in wait for Maceo's invading forces between Coliseo and Lumidero. The Cubans seemed outgeneraled, when it occurred to Maceo to order the firing of the cane fields on either side of the Spaniards. The result of this was that Campos, finding himself between two columns of flame, retreated into Havana on Christmas Day, completely vanquished. His resignation followed at once, and was accepted.

Part of Campos' fame as a general rests upon the building of the trochas. He found them effectual in the last war for fencing the enemy out of certain districts. The trocha is a ditch nine feet deep, filled with water. On each side is a wire fence. On the east bank (always the one toward the insurgents) is a beaten path, patrolled by cavalrymen, and having light artillery defences. On the west side are detached earthworks, guarded by infantry and connected by telephone. Approaches are protected by rifle pits.

In this war a trocha was first built between Puerto Principe and Santa Clara provinces. The insurgents easily evaded it. Another was built through Las Cruces and Las Lajas, but the rebels found their way through that, also. The Spanish retreated still further toward the west, and the capital, and constructed a third trocha from Matanzas to the Bay of La Broa.

The insurgent burning of the sugar fields has been criticised severely by onlookers, and has been held up by the Spanish as an example of the reckless, uncivilized methods of their foes. In reality, it is part of a distinctly planned policy. From the sugar crop Spain receives in peace the largest part of its Cuban revenues. To destroy the crop is to cripple Spain, already nearly bankrupt, and to cripple Spain enough is to make Cuba free, indeed.

General Valeriano Weyler, known in Cuba as "the Butcher," succeeded Campos. He was warmly received in Havana, where he arrived on February 10, 1896. He did not take the field against the rebels until the following November. This was due to the rainy season, which, setting in a few months after his arrival, made fighting impossible until late in the fall.

Maceo was in the western part of Pinar del Rio when Weyler sallied out of Havana, avowedly to crush him. Gomez, in Havana province, he ignored for the time. When he reached Pinar del Rio he met the Cubans in ten engagements in fifteen days. The skirmishes and battles were at Paso Real, Candelario, Rio Hondu, San Cristobal, Neuva Empressa, Guira Melera and Iniquica. In each the Spanish suffered loss. Moreover, they were obliged to swallow the mortification of watching from the rear the victorious advance of the "rebels" toward Havana. They themselves returned to the western part of the island later, and Weyler re-entered the capital.

While Maceo was in Havana province he was killed by the Spanish under Major Cirujada.

General Weyler wrote statements concerning the complete pacification of various provinces of the island, but, in January, 1897, raised some question as to the trustworthiness of his own reports by again leaving Havana to engage in warfare in the "pacified" in-

terior. Again, he gained no advantage whatever, and soon the rainy season forced him to
give up active hostilities.

By the time another dry season had arrived
Weyler was immersed in difficulties with his
home government. In October, 1897, Don
Ramon Blanco, the present Captain General,
was sent to succeed him, and he returned to
Spain. Blanco has, so far, followed the example of his predecessors, and failed to put down
the rebellion.

X.

THE most conspicuous man in the Spanish forces during the present Cuban war has been General Valeriano Weyler y Nicolau, Marquis of Teneriffe. He came widely heralded as "the Butcher." His popular title he gained in the Ten Years' War, where, as a colonel, he had followed the fortunes of Spain. The Cubans told of his cruelty to women and children. His "concentration" policy seemed to lend color to the reports of his foes. His striking personality has been most graphically described by Elbert Rappleye:—

"And what a picture! A little man. An apparition of blacks—black eyes, black hair, black beard—dark, exceedingly dark complexion; a plain black attire, black shoes, black tie, a very dirty shirt and soiled standing collar, with no jewelry and not a relief from the aspect of darkness anywhere on his person. * * *

"His eyes far apart, bright, alert and strik-

ing, took me in at a glance. His face seemed to
run to chin, his lower jaw protruding far beyond any ordinary indication of firmness, per-
sistence or will power.   *   *   *   His nose
is aquiline, bloodless and obtrusive.

"Inferior physically, unsoldierly in bearing,
exhibiting no trace of refined sensibilities, nor
pleasure in the gentle associations that others
live for, he is, nevertheless, the embodiment of
mental acuteness, craft, unscrupulous, fearless
and of indomitable perseverance."

Mr. Rappleye's inference of a cruel nature
expressed by this exterior seems borne out
by occasional reports from the seat of war,
even those making no especial mention of
characteristic "butcher" methods.   One such
dealt chiefly with his escape from death in the
Siguranca mountains in February, 1897.   His
horse was shot under him as he rode to attack
an insurgent hospital!

Weyler says frankly and egotistically of himself:—

"I care not for America, England—any
one—but only for the treaties we have with
them.   They are the law.   *   *   * I know I
am merciless, but mercy has no place in war.
I know the reputation which has been built up

for me. *　*　* I care not what is said about me unless it is a lie so grave as to occasion alarm. I am not a politician. I am Weyler."

Weyler was born forty-nine years ago in Palma, capital of Majorca, one of the Balearic islands.

Campos was a different sort of man, "fat, good natured, wise, philosophical, slow in his mental processes, clear in his judgment, emphatic in his opinions, outspoken and withal lovable, humane, conservative, constructive, progressive, with but one project ever before him—the glorification of Spain as a motherland and a figure among peaceful, enlightened nations."

Campos—Arsenio Martinez Campos—was born in Cuba in 1834. He was educated in Madrid. In 1870 he was a brigadier against the Carlist insurrection. He fought in the Ten Years' War as general and brought it to a close at Zanjon. As Minister of War and Prime Minister in 1879 he tried to redeem his pledges to Cuba, but received no support from his colleagues or the Cortes.

Weyler's successor, Don Ramon Blanco y Erenas, Marquis of Pena Plata, has been all his life a man of war. He won his first renown in the war against the Carlists. In 1879 he was Captain General of Cuba. At Catalonia and in the Philippines he has been governor. His methods are not the lenient ones of Campos, and he himself complacently counts his executions and the hundreds of Philippinian rebels whom he deported to the frightful Spanish colonial jails.

In strong contrast to these leaders and their methods are the leaders of the Cuban cause and their methods. Their commander in chief, Maximo Gomez, says to all his men:—

"Do not risk your life unnecessarily. You have only one and can best serve your country by saving it. Dead men cannot fire guns. Keep your head cool, your machete warm, and we will yet free Cuba."

He is about seventy-five years old. He was born in Santo Domingo. At one time he was a soldier in the Spanish army, serving as a captain under Valeriano Weyler.

He is described by an English writer who joined the insurrectionists in Cuba thus:—

"He is a study in repose or in action. Slender in build, not over one hundred and forty pounds in weight, about five feet seven inches in height, straight as an arrow. His face is tanned; his hair and mustache are iron gray; his cheek bones are prominent and his chin firm. His cool, calculating eyes seem at first completely to measure you, and then the face breaks into a reassuring smile. On the saddle, the horse is a part of him. He never seems to guide it.

"His Spanish love of externals is seen in his superb black stallion, in his faultless uniform, in glittering pistols that hang from his belt, in the gold mounted carbine flung from the pommel of his saddle, in his decorated sabre, and in the grandeur of his manner whenever he comes into contact with somebody from the world without, especially an American."

Not less interesting than "Cuba's champion was the man whom the Spaniards have described as an ignorant negro, Antonio Maceo. He was born in 1843 in Santiago de Cuba. Twenty-three times he was wounded by the Spanish troops in various uprisings. His chest was pierced through and through and his continued existence seemed miraculous. Hatred of the Spanish was with his family a traditional feeling. Six of his brothers died fighting Spain, and one, Filipe, lives an invalid on account of his wounds.

Antonio Maceo in the Ten Years' War reached the rank of major general by the sheer force of his military genius. In this war he outwitted Spain's most renowned generals and defeated with his small, poorly trained forces the flower of the Spanish army. He was killed finally in Havana province in December, 1896, and it will probably never be doubted by his followers that his death was due to the disloyalty of one among his allies.

General Martinez Campos, writing to Spain's Prime Minister in 1878, said of him:—

"It is very difficult to arrange peace in Santiago de Cuba (Zanjon Treaty), where Antonio Maceo rules. He was a peasant, and is now a general. His ambition is enormous, his courage great, his prestige immense among his countrymen. He is a man of high natural talent, and for him nothing could be done, notwithstanding the wishes of the Cuban government."

So far the civil authorities in Cuba have not played so brilliant a part in its history as the military leaders. The first president of the republic established in 1895 was Salvador Cisneros Betancourt, Marquis de Santa Lucia. He was born in Puerto Principe in 1832. It was his privilege to sign the decree abolishing slavery in 1870. He lived in New York from 1878 until 1886 agitating new revolutionary movements. He was in favor of annexation to the United States, a view in which his successor, Bartolome Maso, does not agree with him.

Maso was born in Manzanillo and educated at Havana University. He was a wealthy planter, but he threw aside his fortune to fight in the Ten Years' War. He was imprisoned and deported for denouncing the bad faith of the Spaniards after the Zanjon Treaty. He succeeded Cisneros in October, 1897. According to the constitution of the Cuban Republic, officers of the government serve for two years.

XI.

AFTER the treaty of peace which concluded the Ten Years' War Cuba's right to representation in the Cortes appears to have been recognized. The word "appears" is used advisedly, for Cuba's representatives, exactly calculated, amount to three senators from the province of Havana, one from Santiago and one from the Society of the Friends of the Country. Eight deputies for more than one million of Cubans!

They are further permitted thirty deputies elected by popular ballot, one representative for every 50,000 inhabitants.

The clause "elected by popular ballot" is important, for it may thus be easily understood that the Spanish natives and the Cuban Volunteers expect to influence the elections. That they are successful is evidenced in the fact that last spring out of thirty deputies twenty-six were natives of Spain.

In spite of the Treaty of Zanjon and the

supplementary Act of 1879 Madrid's colonial policy would seem still to be characterized by a system of monopoly and a lack of sincerity.

The head of the military government in Cuba is all powerful. His title is Governor General. In 1825, when Cuba gained the title of "The Ever Faithful Isle," the functions of this personage might have been defined as those of a despot. To-day he may be said to retain the same liberties of action. His appointment is by the Crown and endures for not less than three years and not more than five. Of the civil, ecclesiastical, military and naval organizations he is chief. He is at the head of an army consisting of 13,000 troops, gathered from Spain and salaried out of the Cuban exchequer.

Subject to the Governor General's summons is a body known as the Council of Administration, composed of thirty members. Fifteen are appointed by the Crown, fifteen are elected by the provinces; but, as is customary under Spanish diplomacy, a safe majority of Peninsulars or ultra-loyalists is assured.

The Council of Administration is peculiar, not only in that it serves without pay, but that, being held personally and financially responsible if its votes displease, it is always in danger of being sued for damages. Besides being depended upon to give universal satisfaction it has a number of other duties, among them the preparation of receipts and expenditures for the review of the Cortes and the framing of resolutions on any important public matter. But here, too, the Governor General is all powerful. If he approve these resolutions they pass into effect, if not he holds them over. Indeed, his authority is so supreme that he may suspend such members of the administrative council as are troublesome up to the number of fourteen, or he may even suspend them all after consultation with another body known as the Council of Authorities. He may then proceed, the latter body always, however, apprising the home government of any differences that may disturb his amicable relations with the Council of Administration.

The Council of Authorities is composed exclusively of high dignitaries, the Archbishop of Santiago, the Bishop of Havana, the commanding officers of the army and navy, the chief justice of the Supreme Court of Havana, the Attorney General, the head of the Department of Finances and the director of the local administration.

The Governor General's power extends even to the control of the provinces, each of which is nominally conducted by a Governor of its own, an appointee of the Crown. He has, for instance, the authority to suspend, on the report of the Governor, any of the provincial assemblies, which are elected for a term of four years.

City governments are under the control of a mayor, also subject to removal at the Governor General's pleasure.

Two superior courts are included in the judicial system of Cuba, which are not of overweening importance, since in the Governor General, under a provision of 1878, is vested the power to overrule any decisions of any court, or even to postpone the enactment of any decree proceeding from the government at Madrid.

Assisted by the rector of the University of Havana, like himself a native of Spain, the Governor General has supreme voice in the educational system of Cuba. Besides the University of Havana, there is a collegiate institute in each of the six provinces, where degrees may be conferred. When there is the ability and desire to establish schools, education is compulsory; otherwise, the law of 1880, enforcing education, is ignored.

The laws governing associations and societies are rigid. Their purposes, constitutions and by-laws must be submitted to the governor of the province in which they are organized. He may have the privilege of considering himself an honored guest at their meetings whenever he so desires. Furthermore, he may at his discretion, perhaps because a note of revolution seems to be present, dissolve the assemblage and forbid its meeting again until the superior court of the district has passed upon his judgment.

The governor of each province is vested with the power of censorship over the publication of all literature, and with the Governor General rests full authority to prohibit or permit any pictures or caricatures.

Anonymous publications are absolutely forbidden, no matter how innocent. It is obligatory that three copies of any issue whatsoever be sent to the governor or mayor to be passed upon.

Jews and Protestants are at a discount on

the island. The Roman Catholic is the only religion tolerated, and no one would be permitted to advance doctrines contrary to the established Church, though he would be permitted to live in Cuba and conduct his worship privately.

A provisional government was formed by the insurgents in September, 1895. There were present twenty representatives from all the provinces but Pinar del Rio. They drew up and adopted a constitution and elected officers of state, of whom the President was Salvador Cisneros Betancourt. Bartolome Maso was Vice President, who has since become President.

This government has its seat at Cubitas, on the top of a mountain twenty-five miles from Puerto Principe, but it is in reality a sort of peripatetic committee of affairs, whose authority is largely on paper.

Cuban currency is in a remarkably tangled state. The unit of measure is an ounce of gold, but Spanish gold, being less fine than American, is not worth so much. These two golds and silver circulate confusedly. Paper money is not used.

XII.

CUBA is in the northern part of the torrid zone, just south of Florida. It lies between 74 degrees and 85 degrees west longtitude and 19 degrees and 23 degrees north latitude. It contains 43,314 square miles, an area equal to England, excluding Wales, or one-fourth of Spain. It is twenty-nine times the size of Long Island. Its average breadth is eighty miles. The Island of Pines, the largest of the neighboring islands which belong to it, is 1,214 square miles in area.

According to the last official census in 1887, there were 1,631,687 inhabitants. Of these one-fifth were natives of Spain, 10,500 were whites of foreign blood, 485,187 were free negroes, about 50,000 were Chinese and the rest native Cubans.

The coast is low and flat, and is approached in many parts by islands and reefs. It measures, exclusive of its indentations, 2,200 miles.

Including them, it measures 7,000 miles. It has many admirable and well protected harbors, especially on the north side, where are Havana, Matanzas and Cardenas.

It is as far from the Florida mainland as New York is from Albany.

From Key West to the nearest point on the Cuban coast is 36 miles.

From Key West to Havana is 93 miles.

From New York to Havana is 1,413 miles.

From New Orleans to Havana is 475 miles.

Above the lowlands of the coast rise grazing and farm lands. Four-fifths of the land is a fertile plain. The rest is dense forest land, in which are found rich woods, mahogany, ebony, cedar, palm and granadillo.

The eastern section, especially the province of Santiago de Cuba, is mountainous. In it are found minerals—iron ore, fine steel, gold and silver in small quantities, copper in abundance, fine bituminous coal and marble.

Tobacco and sugar are the chief products and constitute the chief wealth of Cuba, although cotton and coffee are also grown. In Pinar del Rio is raised the finest tobacco in the world.

On the coast the climate is that of the torrid

zone. Inland it is more temperate. In the country districts in the provinces of Matanzas and Havana even the summer period is healthy. In the provinces of Puerto Principe and Santiago de Cuba the character of the country is hilly and the temperature equable. The western part of the island is as habitable as western Pennsylvania.

The simplest precautions and the observance of most ordinary hygienic rules would enable troops to operate in Cuba with no more danger of disease than they would incur in the southern part of the United States. The tropical fruits should be avoided by unacclimated persons. Sugar cane, which, in spite of the destruction of the fields, is still to be found in Cuba, is not ripe until the fall. Earlier in the year it is sweet but very watery, and contains large amounts of glutinous substances conducive to intestinal troubles. Yellow fever exists in Matanzas, Sagua, Havana, Cardenas and Santiago almost continuously. The interior cities, however, are seldom visited by it and it does not exist at all in the country. A mild form of malaria prevails throughout the lowlands. Sunstroke is very uncommon among the natives, but might prevail among recently arrived troops unless they were properly clothed and had frequent opportunities for bathing.

The diet for fresh arrivals in Cuba should consist of plenty of meat, few vegetables, coffee in generous quantities and no alcohol at all.

England advises woollen underwear for her tropical troops and colonists, but those who have lived long in Cuba declare that linen, light both in weight and color, is the proper material for the Cuban climate. Wool is not desirable there because it retains dampness longer than linen, and dampness is one of the conditions which will confront the American troops.

From the first of May until the end of October is the rainy season. This is the only real drawback to the Cuban climate, for its heat and cold are never of the extreme variety and there is only a slight difference between the summer and winter temperatures. The average temperature in Havana in the hottest month is only 81 degrees Fahrenheit, in the coldest only 70 degrees Fahrenheit. Breezes redeem even the rainy season. The average number of rainy days during a month in the rainy season is eight or ten. The rainfall is generally in the afternoon. Earthquakes are of rare occurrence, Santiago de Cuba being more frequently visited by them than any other province.

The official political divisions of the island are Pinar del Rio, the westernmost of the provinces; Havana, Matanzas, Santa Clara, Puerto Principe and Santiago de Cuba, lying east of one another in the order named. Each of these provinces is named from its capital city.

Havana, the chief city of the island, has a fluctuating population of about two hundred thousand. It contains many fine buildings and many squalid ones. To the tourist it is very picturesque. The harbor, if properly dredged, could shelter the navies of the world. Its chief defences are the Castillo de la Punta, on the west of the harbor, and the Castillo de la Morro and San Carlos de la Cabana, to the east. At the head of one arm of Havana bay is the fort which commands both the city and the adjacent country—the Santo Domingo de Atares. The Castillo del Principe is the other principal fortification of Havana.

Second in commercial importance to Havana is Matanzas, which lies about seventy-four miles from Havana, on the northern coast of the island. It has a population of about fifty thousand. It is one of the most beautifully situated cities in Cuba.

Santiago de Cuba is the most flourishing city in the eastern part of the island. It has an admirable harbor, communicating with the sea through a narrow passage. Its most conspicuous defence is called Morro Castle.

The most modern city of importance in Cuba is Cienfuegos, in the province of Santa Clara. It has a population of over twenty-six thousand. Its harbor is one of the best on the southern coast.

Another important city on the northern coast is Cardenas. It is east of Havana about one hundred miles. It has a population of over twenty thousand, has a flourishing trade and large manufactories.

The eastern point of the island is Cape Maisi, and the western Cape St. Antonio. At the western end of the south shore of the province of Santiago de Cuba, opposite Cape Maisi, is Cape Cruz. Between these two capes runs the Sierra Maestra range. The whole eastern part of Santiago de Cuba is mountainous, and broken mountain ranges lie throughout the island.

The Sierra Maestra range changes its name in about the middle of its course, and becomes the Sierra de Cobre, or Copper Mountains. Here is the highest point of land in Cuba— Blue Peak (Pico Turquino), 8,320 feet high.

Rivers are numerous, but not large or often navigable. Many of them "lose themselves." The largest of them is the Cauto, in Santiago de Cuba, which is navigable for fifty miles. The Chorrera, or Almendares, supplies Havana with water. The largest one on the northern coast is the Sagua la Grande, ninety miles long and navigable for twenty miles.

Lakes are comparatively few in Cuba. They lie mainly near the coast swamps, but there are some also in the mountains.

Santiago de Cuba, besides its mountains, has wonderful cascades, caves and cataracts. United States Navy Lieutenant Andrew Rowan, in "The Island of Cuba," says of this province:—

"This extremely broken and precipitous country is the least known, as it is the most difficult of access of any of the political divisions of the island. Roads are few and poor, but the great diversity of products, due to rapid change in the climate, which is caused by the difference in elevation, makes this region one of the most wonderful in the world. The cascades, cataracts and natural portals, surrounded by an ever-verdant foliage, combined with numerous species of flowering orchids and other tropical flowers, and with an animal life in all its gayest colors, present here a picture such as is furnished at but few points on the globe."

XIII.

Notes from the Front.

A LETTER FROM FREDERIC REMINGTON, ON BOARD THE BATTLE SHIP IOWA.

I BOARDED the tug which took all the shore leave men off to their ships and was "landed" (one might almost say it) on the Iowa --battle ship—an iron island floating on the sea.

The Captain was the celebrated Fighting Bob Evans of common report, but aboard ship I found him a calm-eyed man—very plain and straightforward in his affairs. It was Captain Evans simply—and stand up when you say it and have your statement straight, for the weather roll in the Captain's eye as it turns over your person is very severe and not encouraging.

To a shore man the environment of a modern battle ship is more strange than any dream. It cock-tails up in your mind with a nut and bolt factory as a base—but the other mixtures are like an international exhibition, a World's Fair of people and things. The throb of engines—the shrill squeeling of bo'suns' whistles—electric lights—cranes swinging coal in from the lighter 'longside, long guns bigger than forest trees sticking everywhere, sharp orders, gentlemanly officers in white duck trousers, and bare-footed jackies running about, monkey-like in their movements, while marine guards strut martially across the deck.

You go to the dining room—or, as they say, "wardroom"—through another room which makes you chilly because it is filled with long fish-like torpedoes which are loaded with dynamite or other nervous things which are difficult to tolerate on intimate living terms.

And to-morrow we are going to war. One doesn't in these days go to war often enough to make it commonplace, and yet strain as I would, hunt high and low, officers and sailormen, I could find nothing but the most deadly apathy concerning the whole proceeding. I don't think it was because they were overused to going to war, but they have eaten and slept and drilled and thought so much within this

ship's sides that it has eaten up their other
thoughts. They are a part of the big machine
the Iowa, and she was built to go to war—so
why not?

Every one was happy on the fine morning,
going to war. Sailors hate a blockade—they
dread inaction. They want to mix it up with
the batteries, but the blessed old United States
Army is not ready yet, so they must wait; but
they took it out of the soldiers, and dearly I
wished for some of them to be along to take
their own part—for it's no funeral of mine if
the tents, the grub, the mules and the guns are
not there ready for men to use.

"To-morrow may bring great things,"
mused an officer alongside me. "What do
you think—a lieutenant at forty-five years of
age—what do you think?" sighed this har-
rowed soul. "A hero at forty-five years—I
did not enter the service to be a hero at forty-
five years. I told the Secretary a while ago
that when I died all I wanted on my tombstone
was 'Lieutenant B——, U. S. Navy, Bun-
coed.'"

Do not imagine that this deep sentiment in-
terferes with my old friend—he likes to think
aloud about his trouble—and it's a good fash-

ion very much affected by all the seagoing men.

A fat little 'prentice boy became confidential with me after introducing me to many ship's mysteries, and said, "We are starving aboard this ship—we have nothing to eat."

With surprise I turned on him—such a startling statement—to think of Uncle Sam's starving these brave "bullies" of his, but I kept back my laugh, for the fat little rascal was positively greasy, and his trousers strained about his legs.

I can see the Captain up on the bridge, forty feet above the water; the executive, Mr. Rodgers, a sharp visaged gentleman, who goes speeding about the ship hunting up trouble for any man who looks comfortable; and the engineer officers, who come up out of the coal and grease for a breath of fresh air. The marine sergeant in charge of the after deck sweats badly as he strides about, buttoned up to the last gasp. The young officers in the steerage show me a strange Burmah goddess—in marble—kept under lock and key, except when they make their big medicine, and they told me the story, but my lips are ice.

Sometimes things do happen, but they are

little things. The black cat fell overboard one
morning, or the fox terrier who inhabits up
forward chased him overboard—we do not
know which. An alarm was promptly given—
it would never do to have a black cat lose her
life in such a way, for black cats in particular
are portentous things even when alive, but
dead ones are something awful. Who knows
what might happen after that?

So a boat was lowered and the big battle
ship Iowa temporarily abandoned the blockade
of Havana and steamed in a circle, hunting one
lost black cat. The cat came alongside, paw-
ing the water frantically, and was rescued by a
jackie who went down the sea ladder and
grabbed her just in time.

With night it comes cool, and the officers
and men sit smoking in the shadow of the
superstructure, gazing at the lights of Havana
—we might be a yachting party off Newport,
only we are not. The guns are all shotted and
the watch on deck lies about them on the deck,
all ready on the instant. There are two little
tubs of Spanish gunboats in the harbor, which
come outside and are chased back. They appear to be monkeying with us, but if they get
near enough we will saw them off and have
fun with them.

The sea is like the water in your bath tub;
the iron plate of the Iowa is a griddle—the sky
is more red than blue, and a mosquito's wings
would create a hurricane in the air.

A Letter from Julian Hawthorne.

IN India the famine is the result of
natural causes, uncontrollable by
man, and to abate which every effort was made; you felt in looking
at the victims that all was being done for
them that energy and intelligence could do,
and that humanity and science were united in
the effort to succor them.   But in Cuba it is
another story.   These people have starved in
a land capable of supplying tens of millions of
people with abundant food.   The very ground
on which they lie down to breathe their last
might be planted with produce that would feed
them to repletion.   But so far from any effort
to save them having been made by Spain, she
has wilfully and designedly compassed their destruction.   She has driven them in from their
fields and plantations and forbidden them to
help themselves; the plantations themselves
have been laid waste, and should the miserable
reconcentrados attempt under the pretended

kindly dispensation of Blanco to return to
their properties they would find the Spanish
guerillas lying in wait to massacre them.   No
agony of either mind or body has been want-
ing.   The wife has lost her husband, the
mother her children, the child its parents, the
husband his family.   They have seen them die.
Often they have seen them slaughtered wan-
tonly as they lay helpless, waiting a slower end.
The active as well as the passive cruelties of
the Spaniards toward these people have been
well nigh unimaginable.   The stories sent
home by journalists are uniformly within the
truth, for journalists are familiar with human
suffering of all kinds, and are not carried off
their feet by the sight of it.   The comfortable
readers who did not believe a tithe of them at
home, when they have investigated for themselves declare that a tithe has not been told.

JULIAN HAWTHORNE.

A Letter from Robert W. Edgren.

ON the red-hot sand she lay, a
child of seven years—her black
hair matted with blood and dirt,
on her head a ghastly cut made
by a machete.   Overhead the black buzzards

of Cuba soared in lessening circles.   Near at
hand was a poor, palm thatched hut.   At the
very threshold lay the body of another child,
starved and thin.   The machete had been
there, too, and starvation had been robbed of
another victim.   Inside the hut lay a man shot
through the back.   His bloodless face, lying
on the hard earth, his nerveless skeleton hands
grasping in death some poor trinket that the
plunderers had failed to find of sufficient value
to warrant carrying away.   I turned aside sick-
ened.   On his horse sat the Spanish soldier,
our body guard kindly ordered by the com-
mandant to show us the scenery about Mont-
serrat.   In the hot sun his eyes seem to nar-
.row with amusement at the feeling displayed
by those fool "Americanos."   It was a joke to
him.   It amused him to see our looks of hor-
ror, and he showed his wolfish fangs in a grin
of satisfaction.   The bundle of rags that we
had first seen moved a little.   The Red Cross
doctor uttered an exclamation.   In an instant
he was on his knees, and the little girl was carefully lifted in a pair of strong arms and carried
into the shade, and the buzzards flapped their
black wings in silent protest.   Half an hour
later, when the ragged gash had been carefully

dressed and the little patient opened her eyes to look into strange faces the doctor heard her story.

It was not an uncommon one—in Cuba.

"How did you get hurt?"

"Machete."

"Where is your father?"

"Machete; and my sister the soldiers—"

Then her eye caught the figure of our body guard sitting on his horse, machete at his side, and she uttered a faint cry of fear. No other word would she utter. The terror of Spaniards seals tongues in this land of murder and rapine. She is dead now, poor child, but others will take her place. The Spanish soldier will never carry a clean blade while women and children are unprotected.

ROBERT W. EDGREN.

General Fitzhugh Lee's Opinion.

THE Spanish soldiers are living almost from hand to mouth. They have a good many barrels of flour and a good deal of rice and some potatoes, but not a great many, and a little lard; but everything that the town of Havana has received in the last four or five months has been taken from the United States by steamers from New York, New Orleans and Tampa. The Spanish soldiers are badly clothed and very badly fed; not well organized; not drilled. Nobody ever saw Spanish soldiers drill. The same condition of things existed when Mr. Cleveland asked me to go down there last June a year ago. I gave him a report three weeks after I got there, in which I told him there was no chance, in my opinion, of the Spaniards ever suppressing that insurrection, nor was there any chance of the insurrectionists expelling the Spanish soldiers from the island. I have never thought that the insurgents had anything except the skeleton form of a government—a movable capital. I asked them one day why they did not have some permanent capital, and I think they gave a very good reason. They said it would require a large force to protect it and defend it, and that they could not afford to mass up their men there; that the capital and the government officers had to move where they could be safest.

*   *   *   *   *

(A Letter from Grover Flint)

"Were you ever at sea in an open boat, in a tropical ocean, swept by squalls and tornadoes, and travelled only by filibusters and

Spanish cruisers eager for their capture? We were eleven in such a party—three Cuban officers, three Cuban coast pilots, a doctor of the Sanitary Department, a newspaper correspondent and three negro sailors. Our mascot, a green and red parrot, which winked intelligently when the word filibuster was mentioned, and which cried "Al machete! Al machete!" when excited, completed the makeup of the party. Days dragged, and our materials came a little at a time. We lay beneath the palm and wild grape trees, tortured by mosquitoes and sand flies, half a mile from Naternillos Light and the entrance to Nuevitas Harbor. In that harbor lay a gunboat, and another was on duty patrolling the coast for a few miles to east and west of us. Stories came from the town that our expedition was the talk of the cafes, and the bogie of treachery looked nearer to us than we cared at the time to admit. A government commission with state papers and despatches would be no mean capture, and we felt that our heads would fetch a good price!

We were off at last, after twenty days of toil and anxiety. The strain was too great for the little group of watchers on land. Prudence was thrown to the winds and a "Viva!"

rose that a gust caught and carried over the palm trees. "Viva Cuba! Viva la Independencia!" from the shore was answered by a faint "Al machete! Al machete!" from our boat. Then a cloud passed over the moon and we were fairly started on our journey.

Our first course lay due northwest toward Naternillos Light, in order to make the pass in the reefs that lie in front of the entrance to Nuevitas Harbor. We tossed, in darkness, half a mile to seaward of Naternillos Light, and then sighted the light of Nuevitas Harbor. From this point we struck a north-northwesterly course out through the reefs and past the breakers.

The moon came out from beneath the clouds, and we had fears, as we passed the silver path of its reflection, we might be seen from the lighthouse and a gunboat sent after us. We pitched along, constantly shipping cold waves over our starboard bow that drenched us to the skin, but making good time. In an hour we had passed into the darkness beyond the treachery of the moon's rays, and felt a general sense of relief.

It was a rough, gusty night. Once a squall struck us with a heavy fall of rain, and we took

in all sail; but the wind settled down again to
a northeast blow, and we continued on our
course. We felt now that odds were no longer
against our escape, and, though shivering in
our scanty rags, wet and cold and unable to
sleep, we were contented. We all of us had
seen enough of Spanish atrocities to know
what it meant to be captured, and that the
authorities are not anxious for a repetition of
the lingering Competitor trial.

The sun of July 24 rose through banks of
purple clouds over a heavy sea, and a head
wind was still blowing from the northeast.
At noon the heat was blistering. We were off
the Columbus Banks, in English waters. Below we could see a sandy bottom with beds of
brown sponges, and the lead told four fathoms.

Night closed at last, and some of us slept
in spite of the waves that still dashed over us,
while the others kept themselves awake by
bailing out the boat.

At sunrise on the 25th we sighted Green
Key. We landed there to stretch our cramped
limbs at six o'clock, and were welcomed to
English soil by a party of duck shooters from
Nassau."—Grover Flint.

LE MINUZIE
FANNO LA PER-
FEZIONE MA LA
PERFEZIONE NON
È UNA MINUZIA

THE · GILLISS · PRESS ·

UNITED STATES
FLAGS

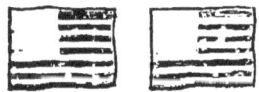

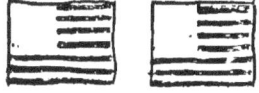

85

GULF
OF MEX

23

COLORADO BANKS

Arroy

Mantua

S. Franc

GUANDIANA BAY

22 CAJON Pt

Melones

Belondron

CAPE
S. ANTONIO

Pt del HOLANDES

CORRIENTES
BAY

CAPE CORRIENTES

DESIGN PATENT APPLIED FOR APRIL 30, 1898, G. H

MAP

A7

Pt de PEÑA AHUJERADA

Camuy

UNITED STATES FLAGS

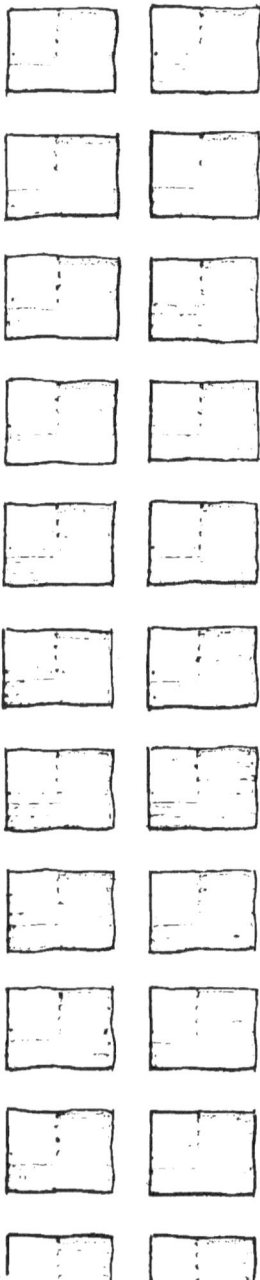

GULF OF MEX

COLORADO BANKS

•Arroy

Mantua•

S.Franc

GUANDIANA BAY

CAJON Pt •Melones

•Belondron

CAPE
S.ANTONIO

CORRIENTES
BAY

Pt del HOLANDES

CAPE CORRIENTES

DESIGN PATENT APPLIED FOR APRIL 30, 1898, G. H

MAP

A

Pt de PEÑA AHUERADA

Camuy

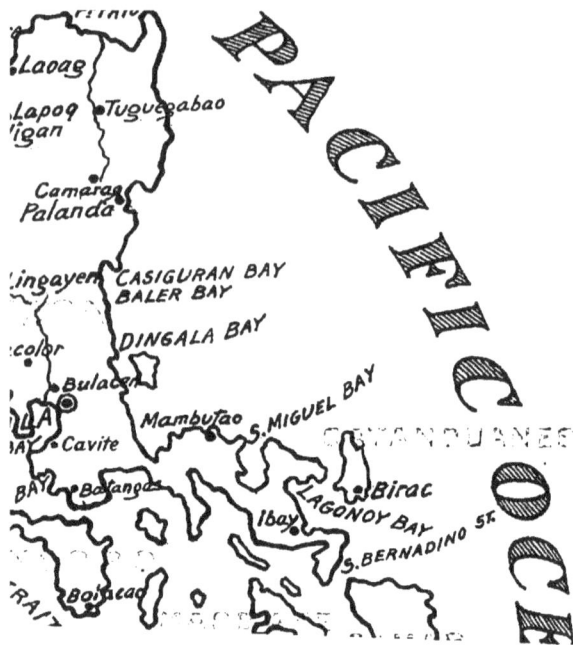

www.ingramcontent.com/pod-product-compliance
Lightning Source LLC
Chambersburg PA
CBHW031441280326
41927CB00038B/1432